# CHIC DECOR DESIGN HOUSE

We hope you enjoy your décor book and the beauty it offers to your space.

Explore other titles in the ALOHA SERIES for complimenting books.

Create your own unique look by mixing and matching with titles from the
BEACH HOUSE SERIES or WOODLAND NATURE SERIES.

If this book added the perfect touch to your interior design plan, we would be
thankful if you could take a quick moment to leave your Amazon Review.

Questions and comments are welcome at chicdecordesignhouse@gmail.com

CHIC DECOR
DESIGN HOUSE

We hope you are enjoying your décor book and the beauty it offers to your space.

If this book added the perfect touch to your interior design plan, we would be thankful if you could take a quick moment to leave your Amazon Review.

Questions and comments are welcome at chicdecordesignhouse@gmail.com